I KNOW AMERICA

Our National Anthem

Stephanie St. Pierre

THE MILLBROOK PRESS

Brookfield, Connecticut

Published by The Millbrook Press
2 Old New Milford Road
Brookfield, CT 06804
© 1992 Blackbirch Graphics, Inc.
First Edition

Created and produced in association with Blackbirch Graphics.
Series Editor: Bruce S. Glassman

Library of Congress Cataloging-in-Publication Data
St. Pierre, Stephanie.
    Our national anthem / Stephanie St. Pierre.
    Includes bibliographical references and index.
    Summary: Examines the history and significance of the national anthem
and several other patriotic songs.
    ISBN 1-56294-106-2
    1. Star-spangled banner (Song)—Juvenile literature. 2. National songs—
United States—History and criticism—Juvenile literature. [1. Star-spangled
banner (Song) 2. National songs—United States.] I. Title. II. Series.
ML3561.S8S78   1992
782.42'1599'0973—dc20   91-38891
                                                                  CIP
                                                                   AC

Acknowledgments and Photo Credits

Cover, back cover. p. 6: North Wind Picture Archives; p. 4: ©Tom Coletti/
The Picture Cube; pp. 7, 16, 34, 35, 39: Library of Congress Collection; pp.
8, 18, 38 (bottom): Bettmann; p. 10: courtesy of Fort McHenry National
Monument and Shrine; p. 11: courtesy of Department of Defense; p. 15:
National Archives; p. 20: courtesy of National Maritime Museum Picture
Library; p. 22: Culver Pictures, Inc,; pp. 24, 29, 30–31: courtesy of the
Maryland Historical Society; p. 32: McLoughlin Bros.; p. 37: ©Bruce
Glassman; p. 38 (top): Smithsonian Institution; p. 40: ©Bob Daemmrich/
Stock, Boston, Inc.; p. 42: courtesy of the U.S. Naval Academy, Annapolis,
Maryland; p. 43: ©Messerschmidt/NFL Photos.

Photo Research by **Inge King.**

CONTENTS

INTRODUCTION

"O say can you see . . ." You hear these words every time you go to a baseball game, or a football game, or maybe every morning in school. Do you know where they came from? They came from a song. It was performed thousands of times all over the United States just last year, not only at baseball and football games, but at hockey games, basketball games, tennis matches, track meets, and lots of other places.

People in huge stadiums stand, take off their hats, place their hands over their hearts, even salute, when the first notes of this famous song blare over loudspeakers. Sometimes it is even sung by someone famous.

Opposite:
The national anthem is sung before the start of a football game.

5

It's the same at small town games and school competitions. And no parade would be complete without this song. All over the world when people hear it they think of the United States of America. The song is, of course, "The Star-Spangled Banner," our national anthem.

What Is a National Anthem?

An anthem is a song of gladness. Most countries have a special song that shows how they feel about their country. That sort of proud song is called a national anthem. The official national anthem of the United States began as a poem written by Francis Scott Key. One night, in 1814, Mr. Key watched an incredible battle between the American militia at Fort McHenry and a mighty fleet of British troops. In the morning, he wrote the poem. Soon it was set to a popular tune and people everywhere were singing it.

For a new country looking for ways to pull its people together and feel proud, "The Star-Spangled Banner" was an inspiration. In 1916, President Woodrow Wilson ordered the army and the navy to play "The Star-Spangled Banner" at all important government gatherings. Finally, more than one hundred years after it was first written, President Herbert Hoover made "The Star-Spangled Banner" the official national anthem. He approved the National Anthem Act of Congress on March 3, 1931.

There are other patriotic songs that Americans like to sing. "Yankee Doodle," "America the Beautiful,"

"The Battle Hymn of the Republic," and "America" are some that are sung often. Over the years, people have thought about making one of these other songs our national anthem. But so far, "The Star-Spangled Banner" is still the favorite.

The story of our national anthem is full of history. It begins at a time when America was still struggling to survive and find an identity. It also begins at a time when the country was at war.

C H A P T E R

THE
STRAIN OF WAR

On June 18, 1812, the United States declared war on Great Britain. It was a brave thing to do. England had the most powerful navy in the world, and the United States was not really prepared for battle at sea or on land. It had only been thirty years since the end of the American Revolution. The country hadn't yet gotten over that war. But many Americans were tired of the problems the British recently had been causing.

War Between England and France

England and France had been at war for a long time. The French Emperor Napoleon wanted to conquer the world. The British wanted to keep control of their

9

The uniforms of three American divisions from the War of 1812: A sergeant in the U.S. Corps of Artillery (left); a corporal in the Baltimore Independent Artilleries (center); a private in the U.S. Sea Fencibles (right).

many colonies and did not want to become part of Napoleon's empire. Both countries hoped to use the New World to improve their positions.

The United States had become an important source of raw materials and goods to the Europeans. The French and the British each wanted to trade with the Americans. But neither wanted to let the other do so. The French would not allow any goods into French territory that came from Britain. They tried to prevent Americans from selling to or buying from the British.

At the same time, the British did not want anyone to sell anything to the French. When they found American ships sailing with goods for the French, they seized the ships and took their cargo.

As the war dragged on, the English began to run short of crewmen and ships to fight the French. Many British sailors were running away from the British Navy and joining the crews of American merchant ships. They were tired of fighting and wanted a new start. But the British wanted their sailors back. They began boarding and searching American ships to find British deserters. If deserters were found, they were forced back to British ships. Sometimes the British also took Americans.

War Between America and Britain

It was bad enough that the British stole cargo from American ships. It was worse when they kidnapped Americans and forced them to fight on British ships.

By the year 1810, the British had seized four thousand sailors. Many of them were American citizens. The Americans decided they had to act. They decided to go to war.

Once the war began, the British forces quickly defeated American troops in many battles. But the

For many years, the British had the largest and most powerful navy in the world.

A LOOK AT THE UNITED STATES IN 1814

At the time that Francis Scott Key wrote the "Star-Spangled Banner," the United States of America was only thirty-eight years old.

Although there were only eighteen states, America had grown enormously since the Revolution. In 1805, President Jefferson bought the Louisiana Territory from Napoleon. Adding this land to the country made it more than twice as big as it had been before. The United States now stretched from the Atlantic Ocean far into the middle of the continent.

The eighteen states that were members of the Union in 1814 were Connecticut, Delaware, Georgia, Kentucky, Louisiana, Maryland, Massachusetts, New Hampshire, New Jersey, New York, North Carolina, Ohio, Pennsylvania, Rhode Island, South Carolina, Tennessee, Vermont, and Virginia.

The biggest cities were Boston, New York, Philadelphia, and Baltimore. Washington, D.C., the nation's capital, was still being built.

The total United States population in all eighteen states was about seven million people. (About that many people live in New York City today.)

More than half of those people either had been born in England or had parents who were born there. Most of the rest came from various places on the European continent.

Most Native Americans were not counted as citizens of the United States, and so the number of Indians living in the states at that time was not recorded. The many black people who were brought to the United States as slaves were not considered citizens either, and so their number was not included in the total population.

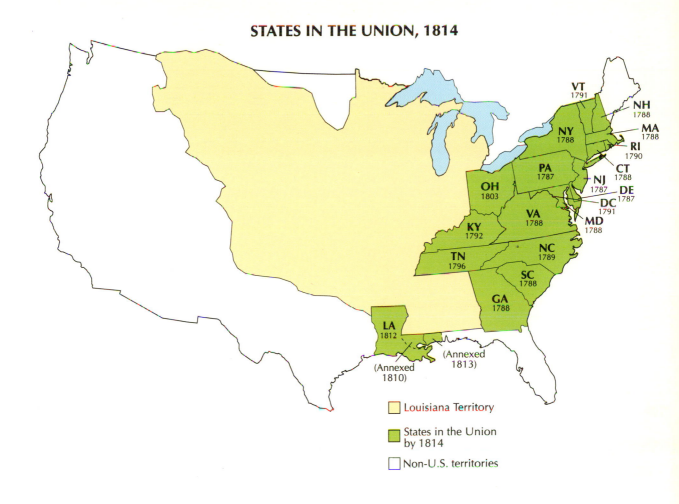

STATES IN THE UNION, 1814

VT 1791
NH 1788
MA 1788
NY 1788
RI 1790
PA 1787
CT 1788
NJ 1787
DE 1787
OH 1803
DC 1791
VA 1788
MD 1788
KY 1792
NC 1789
TN 1796
SC 1788
GA 1788
LA 1812
(Annexed 1813)
(Annexed 1810)

Louisiana Territory

States in the Union by 1814

Non-U.S. territories

Americans had some surprising successes. The British were still at war with France's Napoleon. Most of their attention was given to fighting the French. Sometimes the Americans were able to beat the British in a battle because the British didn't have enough soldiers to fight two wars so far apart at the same time.

The War of 1812, as it was called, went on for over two years. In April of 1814, England's war with France ended. Napoleon was defeated. Now the English could pay more attention to the difficult time they were having in the "colonies," as they still sometimes called the United States. In August of 1814, a huge fleet of British ships entered Chesapeake Bay, off the coast of Maryland. They planned to crush the colonial troublemakers and solidify their power in the New World once and for all.

The Mighty Power of Great Britain

Unlike the British troops, who were professional soldiers, the American troops included many ordinary men who volunteered to fight because they loved their country. They were called the militia. They did not have the same training or experience as the British soldiers. They didn't have as many weapons as the British. But they were heroic and determined to win their battle for justice and freedom.

Not surprisingly, when the British soldiers began their attack, it didn't take them long to defeat the small American militia and capture Washington, D.C., the new capital city. The British quickly burned the Capitol building, the president's house, and many other impor-tant government buildings. It was a terrible setback for the United States. Baltimore, the country's third largest city and an important port, was where the British fleet was headed next.

Opposite:
In 1814, British soldiers attacked Washington, D.C., and burned the Capitol building and the president's house, among other government buildings.

C H A P T E R

2

BY THE DAWN'S EARLY LIGHT

By the time the British reached Baltimore, American troops were ready for them. Americans were angered by the British destruction of their capital city and were determined to hold fast against the invaders. The Americans had strengthened their defenses around the city. They had also strengthened their defenses at Fort McHenry, on the Patapsco River, near Baltimore. Old ships were placed in the shallow river ready to be sunk at a moment's notice. The sunken ships would make it impossible for the large, powerful vessels in the British fleet to use the main channel of the river that led straight to the city.

Opposite:
Francis Scott Key watches the battle at Fort McHenry from a ship on September 13, 1814.

17

An American Strategy Works

On September 11, 1814, the British fleet arrived at the mouth of the Patapsco River. The next day, some of the British soldiers left their ships and began marching toward Baltimore. As the troops came closer to the city, they met up with the American militia. There was much fighting. The British expected an easy victory, but this time they weren't going to get it. In one of the early battles, an important British commander, General Ross, was killed. The battle raged on.

In the meantime, the rest of the British forces were preparing for what would be a historic battle at Fort McHenry. The Americans had sunk twenty-four ships in the channel to block the passage of the British ships upriver. The river was too shallow for most of the British fleet's large ships. But sixteen smaller ones were able to get to within two miles of Fort McHenry.

At dawn on September 13, the battle began. All day and all that night, rockets were shot from the British ships at Fort McHenry. The fort answered with rockets, cannons, and guns of

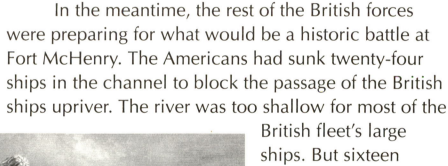

British general Robert Ross was killed in an early battle near Baltimore on September 12, 1814.

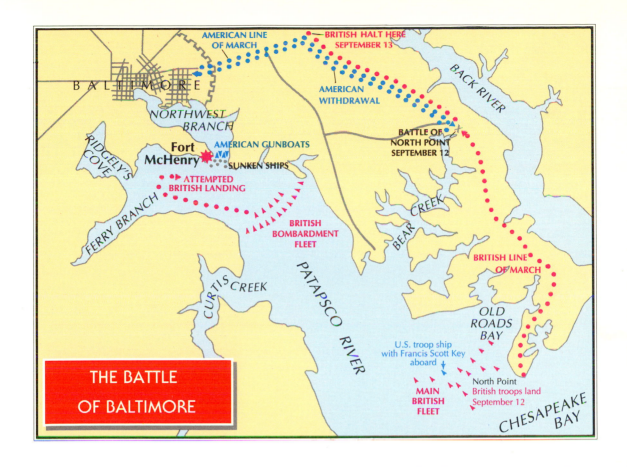

THE BATTLE
OF BALTIMORE

its own. The sky was full of flashing light and smoke. The sound of thunder filled the air. It was hard to tell who was winning the battle. The bombardment went on and on and on.

Francis Scott Key at Fort McHenry

Francis Scott Key was thirty-five years old in 1814. He was a lawyer. He also enjoyed writing poetry. So what was he doing at the battle of Fort McHenry? He was rescuing a friend from the British! When the British

19

had left Washington, D.C., after destroying the city, they had arrested Dr. William Beanes. The doctor had interfered in military matters and caused some British soldiers to be captured. The British planned to take Dr. Beanes to Halifax, in Nova Scotia—at that time still a British colony—for a trial. Francis Scott Key heard about the trouble his friend was in. He asked the president, James Madison, for help in saving the doctor from the British. Soon Key was racing on horseback toward Baltimore with a letter from the president asking for the release of Dr. Beanes.

Somehow Key had to catch up with the British fleet. A U.S. agent named John S. Skinner helped him. In a small ship flying a white flag of truce, they approached the British flagship. The flagship was the head ship of the fleet, where Dr. Beanes was being held prisoner. Key met with the commander of the fleet, Admiral Cochrane, and asked for the release of his friend. But the admiral refused.

Then Key told the admiral how Dr. Beanes had helped many wounded British soldiers. Key even had letters from the soldiers saying how good the doctor had been to them. Finally, the admiral decided to free Dr. Beanes. But he would not allow the Americans to return to Baltimore until after the battle. They had seen and heard too much of the British fleet's plan of attack. And so, from their small ship anchored within sight of the tremendous battle, Key, Skinner, and Dr. Beanes watched as the British continued their attack on Fort McHenry.

FORT McHENRY TODAY

The fort that inspired Francis Scott Key to pen the national anthem is now a national monument and historic shrine. The War of 1812 was the final time guns were fired in anger by the fort. It was last used as a working fort to house soldiers during the Civil War (1861–1865). During that war, political prisoners were kept at the fort. They were civilians (people who aren't soldiers) who tried to help the South. Until the end of World War II in 1945, the fort was used by the military. Then it was used as a Coast Guard training center. Now Fort McHenry is a museum and a park.

There is a lot for visitors to see at Fort McHenry. There are

displays of uniforms from the War of 1812 and the Civil War. Pictures show how the fort looked long ago. In the barracks, rooms are set up just as they were when soldiers lived in them. You can learn about the life of a soldier at the fort and see how he spent his time working and relaxing. There is also a movie about the War of 1812 as seen through the eyes of Dr. William Beanes.

For more information about Fort McHenry, call (301) 962-4299 or write:

The Superintendent
Fort McHenry National
   Monument and Historic
   Shrine
Baltimore, Maryland 21230

C H A P T E R

3

IN
FULL GLORY

Throughout the night, as rockets glared and bombs blasted, Francis Scott Key wondered who was winning the fierce battle. It was hard to tell from his ship in the Chesapeake Bay. Thousands of pounds of shells were fired. But finally, at dawn the next morning, the fighting was over. Clouds of smoke drifted across the water and hung over the battered fort. An eerie quiet settled over the scene. The air still smelled of ignited gunpowder. Key strained his eyes to see the fort. A flag flew above it, but Key couldn't tell if it was the British Union Jack or the American banner. Then, suddenly, a gust of wind unfurled a flag covered with stars and stripes!

Opposite:
The original flag that flew at Fort McHenry in 1814 can still be seen at the Smithsonian Institution in Washington, D.C.

The British Retreat

The Americans had held the fort. The British had given up. Unable to make any dent in the American defenses, the British ships retreated.

The British soldiers on land could not hope to succeed without the troops coming from the sea. They, too, retreated. The next day, the entire British fleet and all its troops headed out into the Atlantic Ocean. The attempt to capture Baltimore had failed! And just as it had during the Revolution, the courage of the American forces saved the day.

The fighting had been non-stop. But just four American soldiers were killed, and only twenty-four others were wounded. It was an amazing victory for

Francis Scott Key was inspired by the American flag when he saw that it had survived the long bombardment of shells and rockets from British troops.

STARS AND STRIPES FOREVER

The flag that Francis Scott Key saw flying over Fort McHenry in 1814 still exists, although it is worn and tattered. You can see it at the Smithsonian Institution in Washington, D.C.

The flag is very large—thirty feet wide by forty-two feet long. That's almost the size of half a basketball court! There are fifteen stripes (eight red and seven white) and fifteen stars on the flag. There is a stripe and a star for each state that was in the Union in 1794.

The flag was made in the summer of 1813 by Mary Young Pickersgill of Baltimore. It was sewn from a cotton material called bunting and cost Fort McHenry $405.90, which was a very large amount of money in those days.

Today the house in which Mary Pickersgill lived is a museum called the Flag House. Many famous flags are displayed there. There are even a few pieces from the tattered Fort McHenry flag at the museum.

In 1971, Fort McHenry had a new flag made. It was made to look exactly like the famous one that flew there in 1814.

the Americans. The sight of the flag blowing in the wind at that moment inspired Key to write a few lines of poetry on the back of an envelope he was carrying. Later that night, safe in his hotel in Baltimore, Key sat down to finish the poem. He called it "The Defense of Fort McHenry." We call it "The Star-Spangled Banner."

Soon after finishing his poem, Francis Scott Key showed it to his brother-in-law, Judge Nicholson. Nicholson liked the poem so much that he arranged to have it printed right away. A few days later, some local papers printed "The Defense of Fort McHenry." A month later, it was set to music and sung after the performance of a play in a Baltimore theater. For the first time, in the theater program, the song was called "The Star-Spangled Banner."

Adding the Music

No one knows for sure who decided on the tune for "The Star-Spangled Banner." It might have been Judge Nicholson. It might have been Francis Scott Key himself. The tune was that of a traditional English song called "To Anacreon in Heaven." It was about drinking ale and being in love. It was a very old song that had been popular in America and England for a long time.

By the time it became "The Star-Spangled Banner," the tune of "To Anacreon in Heaven" had been used for at least eighty-five other American songs, including another one by Key. Nine years earlier, Francis Scott Key had written a poem called "When the Warrior Returns" and set it to the tune. One of the lines from that poem is "By the light of the star-spangled flag." If that sounds familiar, it's because Key used a line very much like it in his later poem: "O, say does that star-spangled banner yet wave. . . ."

Understanding the National Anthem

Often, when you sing a song you don't think too much about what the words mean. Our national anthem is full of images of the heroic deeds of early Americans.

GLOSSARY FOR THE ANTHEM

Learning some new words may help you to understand the "Star-Spangled Banner" better. Look at the words and phrases on this list and then read the verses of the song that follow on the next page.

banner: flag
twilight's last gleaming: sunset, just before dark (**gleaming:** shining)
perilous: dangerous
o'er: over
ramparts: mounds of earth built around a fort to make it stronger
gallantly: bravely, heroically
foe's haughty host: the proud British enemies
dread: frightening
reposes: sits
fitfully: off and on
conceals: hides

discloses: shows
morning's first beam: dawn
vauntingly: proudly, boastfully
havoc: destruction
foul footstep's pollution: ugly trace of the British
refuge: safe place
hireling: hired worker
terror of flight: retreat
towering steep: top of the fort
gloom of the grave: death
triumph: victory
doth: does
desolation: destruction
victr'y: victory, winning
hath: has
preserved: saved, kept
when our cause it is just: when we fight for the good and fair things in the world
motto: saying

If you read the poem carefully, you will see that the "Star-Spangled Banner" has a lot to say about what America means. It shows how important freedom was to the brave Americans who were fighting to start a new nation. We usually sing only the first verse, but all four verses have something to say about patriotism and heroism.

THE STAR-SPANGLED BANNER

O say can you see by the dawn's early light
  What so proudly we hail'd at the twilight's last gleaming,
Whose broad stripes and bright stars through the perilous fight
   O'er the ramparts we watch'd, were so gallantly streaming?
   And the rocket's red glare, the bombs bursting in air,
   Gave proof through the night that our flag was still there,
O say does that star-spangled banner yet wave
O'er the land of the free and the home of the brave?

On the shore dimly seen through the mists of the deep,
  Where the foe's haughty host in dead silence reposes,
What is that which the breeze, o'er the towering steep,
  As it fitfully blows, half conceals, half discloses?
   Now it catches the gleam of the morning's first beam
   In full glory reflected now shines in the stream
'Tis the star-spangled banner—O long may it wave
O'er the land of the free and the home of the brave!

And where is that band who so vauntingly swore,
  That the havoc of war and the battle's confusion
A home and a Country should leave us no more?
  Their blood has wash'd out their foul footstep's pollution.
   No refuge could save their hireling and slave
   From the terror of flight or the gloom of the grave,
And the star-spangled banner in triumph doth wave
O'er the land of the free and the home of the brave.

O thus be it ever when freemen shall stand
  Between their lov'd home and the war's desolation!
Blest with vict'ry and peace may the heav'n rescued land
  Praise the power that hath made and preserv'd us a nation!
   Then conquer we must, when our cause it is just,
   And this be our motto—"In God We Trust,"
And the star-spangled banner in triumph shall wave
O'er the land of the free and the home of the brave.

The First Verse

The first verse of the song is about the bombardment of Fort McHenry. It describes how the sky looked, full of exploding rockets, and how the American flag looked waving above the fort throughout the battle. The fact that the flag "was still there" meant that the Americans had not been beaten. And it meant that America was still free of British rule. Americans could feel proud of their victory.

The Second and Third Verses

The second verse of the song describes the British fleet defeated, watching as the American flag waves proudly and gloriously over Fort McHenry. The third verse is about the way the British bragged that they would defeat the Americans. But instead of destroying the "land of the free and the home of the brave," the British have been destroyed.

The Final Verse

The last verse expresses a hope. It asks that whenever people stand up for the good of their nation, they will defeat their enemies. It is also like a prayer praising the powers that helped Americans to stay together and fight for what they believed in. Americans fought to make their world a better place. Because of that, they had to win.

The next time you sing or hear the national anthem, you can think about what it really means and what it says about America.

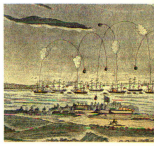

Fort McHenry fell under siege on the memorable night of September 13, 1814.

O' say, can ye see by

What so proudly we hail'd

Whose bright stars & broad stripes, th

O'er the ramparts we watch'd

And the rocket's red glare, the bom-

bone proof through the night that o

O' say does that star-spangle

O'er the land of the free &

Our that shone, dimly seen thro

Where the foe's haughty host in d

What is that which the breeze, o'er

As it fitfully blows, half-conce

Now it catches the gleam of t

the dawn's early light

by the twilight's last gleaming?

rough the clouds of the fight,

were so gallantly streaming?

bursting in air

flag was still there.

banner yet wave

the home of the brave?

ough the mists of the deep,

silence reposes,

the towering steep,

als, half discloses?

morning's first beam,

The words to "The Star-Spangled Banner" in Francis Scott Key's original handwriting.

When Key saw the American flag waving the morning after the battle at Fort McHenry, he was filled with patriotic inspiration. He quickly wrote down a few lines to a poem on the back of an envelope. This poem would later become the words to "The Star-Spangled Banner."

Notice in this version that a few of the words are different from the ones we sing today. The third line reads, "Whose bright stars and broad stripes, through the clouds of the fight..." The version we sing says, "Whose broad stripes and bright stars, through the perilous fight..."

31

C H A P T E R

4

A SONG BECOMES
AN ANTHEM

Right away Americans came to think of "The Star-Spangled Banner" as their national anthem. It was performed often at many different events because by the end of 1814 Americans were feeling very patriotic. They had won the War of 1812 and had defeated the British for the second time in less than forty years.

As time passed, "The Star-Spangled Banner" continued to be one of the country's most popular songs. Each year, it was played more and more often. But proud Americans yearned to have other songs that celebrated their country's greatness. Over the years many other popular patriotic songs were written. Many of the songs have interesting histories of their own.

Opposite:
A "Yankee Doodle Dandy" rides a pony in an old drawing by Thomas Nast.

33

THE FIRST NATIONAL ANTHEM?

One of the earliest and most popular patriotic American songs was "Yankee Doodle." It was written sometime about the year 1750. No one is really sure who wrote the song but, like many other songs of the time, it was a British song. In fact, the British sang it to make fun of Americans.

In England, it was an insult to call someone a "Yankee Doodle." It was a way of making fun of how shabbily Americans dressed. Americans looked sloppy compared to the British Redcoats in their fancy uniforms. But Americans took pride in their country and even in their shabbiness. They did not want to be at all like the British.

At the end of the American Revolution, the British surrendered at the Battle of Yorktown. George Washington's men played "Yankee Doodle" to show how proud they were of themselves and to show the British general Lord Cornwallis how little they cared if the British made fun of them. After all, Americans had defeated the most powerful army in the world and won their freedom!

"America," by Samuel Francis Smith, is another famous patriotic song. Strangely enough, the music to this song is the same as the tune "God Save the Queen," the British national anthem.

"America the Beautiful"

"America the Beautiful" is one of the most popular patriotic songs, even today. In fact, it almost became our national anthem instead of "The Star-Spangled Banner." It was written in 1895 by Katherine Lee Bates. While visiting Colorado, Miss Bates saw the spectacular view from the mountains and was inspired to write a poem about America's natural beauty. When she went home to Massachusetts, she had the poem printed up on the Fourth of July!

The music of "America the Beautiful" was written by Samuel A. Ward. Originally, the music was for a church song called "Materna." But the music fit the new poem so well that it became "America the Beautiful" from then on.

Many people tried to get Congress to adopt "America the Beautiful" as America's official national anthem. Even today, some people would like to see it replace "The Star-Spangled Banner" for the simple reason that it is a much easier song to sing.

War Songs and Marches

Many patriotic songs have been written during wars to keep people's spirits up. And the armed forces have always had marches to parade to. Some of these have been very popular. The Civil War gave us "The Battle Hymn of the Republic" and "When Johnny Comes Marching Home." Of the military marches, "The Marines' Hymn" (which begins "From the halls of

George M. Cohan wrote many patriotic songs during World War I that inspired both troops and civilians. A statue of Cohan stands in Times Square, New York City, in the heart of Broadway.

Montezuma. . .") has always been popular. Like "The Battle Hymn," it is a very dramatic song to march to.

Two popular songs from World War I were written by George M. Cohan. He was a very talented songwriter and composer. He was also a very proud and patriotic American. (He was born on July 3 but liked to say that he was "born on the Fourth of July.") Cohan created many songs and Broadway shows that celebrated America and all it stands for. One of these shows had a song that used some of the words and

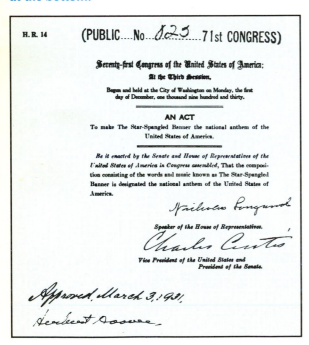

music of the old "Yankee Doodle." It was known as "Yankee Doodle Dandy," and became a big favorite when America got involved in World War I. He also wrote a song especially about the war called "Over There."

Many of these songs became very popular. But "The Star-Spangled Banner" was thought to be the most American of American songs. In 1916, President Woodrow Wilson ordered the army and the navy to play "The Star-Spangled Banner" at all important gatherings.

America's Official Anthem

During the Great Depression of the 1930s, many Americans lost their jobs. This caused some people to become saddened by life in America. The time was right to do something that would unite the country. On March 3, 1931, President Herbert Hoover signed the National Anthem Act of Congress into law. With that, "The Star-Spangled Banner" officially became America's national anthem.

The
Star Spangled Banner

NATIONAL SONG.

"O LONG MAY IT WAVE
OE'R THE LAND OF THE FREE.
AND THE HOME OF THE BRAVE."

SONG OR DUET

with CHORUS Ad Libitum.

Pr: 25 Cnett.
Piano Arrangement - 25

NEW YORK.
Published by WILLIAM DRESSLER, 933 Broadway.

FREEDOM
SHALL STAND

The national anthem is usually performed at the opening of important public events. It serves as a way to unite a crowd or an audience. It reminds everyone that they all belong to one nation. Sporting events, parades, and important school programs are all special occasions that begin with the anthem. There are a few important things to know about listening to the national anthem. There are certain ways that you are expected to act when it is performed. For instance, you should stand up and put your hand on your heart. You should not laugh or talk while the anthem is being performed. Singing along with the performer is, most of the time, acceptable.

Opposite:
Students in south Texas recite the Pledge of Allegiance and sing the national anthem before classes begin.

41

Showing Respect for the Anthem

There have been times when someone has done something that makes people angry while the anthem is performed. Once, at the Olympics, some men who had won Olympic medals did not put their hands on their hearts when the anthem was played. Instead, they gave a special salute. The athletes were black and they saluted in a way that showed their pride in their race. Some people were very upset about this. But the athletes were not disrespectful toward the anthem. They chose to honor it in a way that said something more about their feelings for America.

Another time, a comedian who was performing the anthem at the opening of a baseball game made fun of "The Star-Spangled Banner" while she was singing. She was singing badly and acting in a crude way. People all over the country were upset. Later, the woman apologized for her behavior.

At another time, a rock singer from Ireland refused to have her concert open with "The Star-Spangled Banner." Again, many people were angry. This woman did not make fun of the anthem or act in a bad way, but she did not want patriotic songs about any country sung at her concerts. After a while, most people accepted the fact that a non-American may not want our national anthem sung. In America, even if we do not like what people say or do, everyone has the right to freedom of speech. That means we can all say how we feel about things.

SINGING THE ANTHEM AT SHEA STADIUM

Have you ever wondered how people are chosen to sing the national anthem at a baseball game? At Shea Stadium in New York, the home of the New York Mets, there is a special group of people called the promotion department, who choose the singers and performers and help them do a good job.

Anyone who wants to perform the anthem at a game must send a letter and a tape recording of his or her singing to Shea. The promotion department people listen to the tapes and decide who will sing. Sometimes famous people send in tapes —rock singers like Billy Joel, for instance. Sometimes the people who sing are not very famous. But the promotion department always tries to find people who will do a good job.

It takes from one minute and ten seconds to one minute and forty-five seconds to perform "The Star-Spangled Banner." Sometimes singers or musicians try to make the song fancier or jazzier. The longest it ever took anyone to perform the anthem at Shea Stadium was two minutes and twenty-five seconds. That might not sound like a lot, but it's almost twice as long as usual!

Sometimes there are mix-ups or problems when a performer is ready to go. To make sure that the microphone is working, the performer always speaks to the crowd. That way, if the microphone is too low or too loud, it can be adjusted before the singing, not while the singer is trying to do a good job on the anthem.

It is hard to sing in a big stadium. Because of the microphones and the huge space, singers cannot hear themselves. It takes a few seconds for sound to travel from the microphone and out over the speakers after the singer has sung. Once a young girl, only nine years old, was singing the anthem. She sang the opening line and then stopped. She could not hear her voice over the speakers. She had forgotten the directions of the promotion people. They had told her to keep singing no matter what she heard or didn't hear. Suddenly, she remembered and, despite a longer-than-usual pause, the song sounded fine.

Remembering Francis Scott Key

The man who wrote our national anthem is considered one of our country's true patriots. There are many ways in which he is remembered. There are only eleven places in the United States where the flag is permitted to fly twenty-four hours a day. One of those special places is the birthplace of Francis Scott Key. Another site is at his grave. And still another is at Fort McHenry, where Francis Scott Key was first inspired to write our anthem.

Around 1940, the house that Key lived in was torn down because a bridge was being built between Virginia and Georgetown in Washington, D.C. The bridge was named the Key Bridge. Plans are under way to create a memorial park very close to the spot where Key's house stood. The Francis Scott Key Foundation will oversee the creation of the memorial and hopes to build a museum as well. In addition, the foundation will give scholarships to especially patriotic individuals and to students who are interested in studying the history of the War of 1812.

Like many other American institutions, the Key Foundation works hard to keep the history of our national anthem alive. They know that knowledge of our history creates pride in our heritage. They know that the story of Fort McHenry and Francis Scott Key is an important piece of our country's past. Learning the history of "The Star-Spangled Banner" is just one way in which we can all better understand our common heritage and what it means to be American.

Chronology

June 18, 1812 The United States declares war on Great Britain.

April, 1814 The British defeat France, allowing them to devote more troops to fighting the Americans.

September 11, 1814 A large British fleet arrives in Chesapeake Bay, just outside of Baltimore; troops begin to march toward Baltimore, and are met by American resistance.

September 13, 1814 British ships attack Fort McHenry in the Battle of Baltimore. Francis Scott Key witnesses the battle from a British ship and is inspired to write "The Defense of Fort McHenry," the poem that later becomes the national anthem.

1916 President Woodrow Wilson orders the military to play "The Star-Spangled Banner" at all important gatherings.

March 3, 1931 President Herbert Hoover signs the National Anthem Act of Congress, making "The Star-Spangled Banner" the official national anthem of the United States.

For Further Reading

Bosco, Peter I. *The War of 1812*. Brookfield, Connecticut: The Millbrook Press, 1991. *Explains the causes of the conflict and examines the events surrounding the war. Specific battles are discussed, including the famous bombardment of Fort McHenry.*

Miller, N. *The Star-Spangled Banner*. Chicago: Childrens Press, 1990. *A history of the words and music of our national anthem. Explores the life and work of Francis Scott Key and traces the origins of the music that was paired with his famous poem.*

Osinski, Alice. *Woodrow Wilson*. Chicago: Childrens Press, 1990. *A biography of the president who brought the anthem official government recognition.*

Stein, R.C. *The Burning of Washington*. Chicago: Childrens Press, 1990. *A specific discussion of the events that led up to the battle at Fort McHenry. Explains why the burning of the city did so much to rally American forces and how it ultimately led to their victory.*

Index

47